"RockBottom Has A Basement"

THE FOUNDATION OF ALL THINGS NEW

KIRBY D. GANT II

ROCKBOTTOM HAS A BASEMENT

THE FOUNDATION OF ALL THINGS NEW

KIRBY D. GANT II

Unless otherwise noted, all scriptures were taken from *King James Bible*. (2017). King James Bible Online. https://www.kingjamesbibleonline.org/ (Original work published 1769) and New International Version. (2011). Blue Letter Bible. https://www.blueletterbible.org/niv/index.cfm (Original work published 1973)

ISBN: 979-8-9894295-5-4

Printed in the U.S.A. by
Dr. Kirby Speaks

Table of Contents

ACKNOWLEDGEMENT

I want to take this moment and acknowledge every person who purchased the book. I thank you from the bottom of my heart. I pray this book will strengthen and empower you, as you take the time to read it.

DEDICATION

Surviving a life crisis isn't an easy thing. Most times, many succumb due to the absence of family, friends, support, and love.

Going through is one thing, but it's another thing when going through, and you're surrounded with genuine physical presence, wrapped in real love.

I dedicate this book to my mother, Mrs. Ethel Smalls Brown. You're the epitome of what a mother is. You've always gone the extra mile to make sure your children were taken care of. You stood back and watched your son weather a tough year last year. Your words were always on time. Your sensitivity is undeniable. You're quick and sharp.

I call you blessed. Thank you for being my Rock & Refuge. I love you beyond infinity!

Proverbs 31:28

"Her children arise up, and call her blessed; her husband also, and he praiseth her."

FOREWORD

Warm tears streamed down my face, my eyes swollen, and the inescapable dam of pain burst forth. I did everything in my power to stop the stream… but I could not. The kind voice on the other end of the phone was familiar. It was peaceful. It was filled with love. It was my wife, and her encouraging words cut straight through the noise: *let it out.*

You need to understand something about me before you understand what that moment meant. I have stood at the graveside of family members and never shed a tear. I have sat in the middle of intense board meetings during full-blown organizational crises and never once flinched. If you needed a leader who was ironclad and immovable under pressure, I was your man. Tears were not in my vocabulary. Weakness was not in my world.

So, what was unfolding in that airport was so foreign to me that it felt like it was happening to someone else. I was mortified that it was playing out in front of strangers. I was angry… genuinely angry… that I was having this reaction at all. And on some deep subconscious level, standing in the middle of a crowded airport with tears streaming down my face felt like the least masculine thing that could possibly be happening to me. I was a preacher. A builder. A leader of leaders. And I was falling apart at the seams in a terminal in Africa.

I was walking through that airport on my way home from a whirlwind ministry tour, carrying a weight I had not yet fully named. After nearly two decades of pouring my life into the first church I had ever planted, I had handed it to someone I trusted completely, freeing myself to travel the world and preach the gospel. While I was thousands of miles away, he called to tell me he was leaving… and I later discovered he had already announced a new church plant across town. What I thought was a succession became a master betrayal, and I was standing in that airport holding all of it.

We all have moments in life when it seems as though hope may be lost. This was mine.

I wept tears so deep they traced all the way back to the rugged and painful pathways of my childhood. What I could not see in that moment was that this moment held the key to a new beginning and a fresh start.

Because of the pain I had faced from childhood forward, I had learned to become a professional at living numb. But how do you let something out when you have lived your entire life keeping it all in? This, in essence, was a major part of the problem. In that moment, I chose healing. In that moment, I chose grace. In that moment, I chose a pathway of redemption. I wept tears that not only contained the deepest despair but were also filled with hope for a brighter tomorrow.

The truth is, as men, we are conditioned from boyhood to measure our worth by our output. What we build. What we provide. What we achieve. Nobody pulls a young man aside and teaches him how to simply *be*… they teach him how to *do*. And so, we spend decades stacking accomplishments like armor, never realizing that underneath all of it is a man who has never been properly introduced to himself. This contributes to the lie of living numb.

I had lived under that lie my entire life. What seemed like my darkest moment became one of my brightest. God anchored my mind with these words:

> *"And we know that all things work together for good to them that love God, to them who are the called according to his purpose." Romans 8:28*

I began to lean heavily on the sovereignty of God. I began to realize that every season holds a lesson... some just have to be hunted for. As men, we are innately hunters! What would it look like if we learned to hunt for the lesson in the most painful moments? What would it look like if we found the hand of God in moments of tragedy and trial? This was my journey. This was my lesson.

For the first time in my adult life, I found myself sitting in a chair, talking to a therapist. I was accustomed to being the one conducting the counseling session... not receiving it. Sitting on the other side of that desk, I felt naked and exposed. Vulnerable in a way I had never allowed myself to be. And as uncomfortable as that was, it was exactly what I needed. This man was different. He was not in my church world or ministry circles. He had no preconceived impression of who I was. He simply saw the man in pain who was also filled with potential. He confronted weaknesses, exposed vulnerabilities, and offered profound steps of healing.

That was several years ago, and today I am a different person! My basement experience became the beginning of an ascension. An ascension not just into being a great leader and an accomplished entrepreneur, but into being a complete, whole, and wise man. I can now look back at what seemed like the worst moment of my life in ministry and realize it was a great gift. I would have never pursued the pathway of healing had I not stumbled through that moment. Granted, it was awkward. It was difficult. But it was necessary.

Men… I want you to know your value is not in what you do! I want you to know that you were valued before you ever came into human form. Your loving Father God, the Creator of heaven and earth, designed you for a destiny and a purpose. There is grace in your struggle. There are lessons in your valleys. There are gifts in the setbacks. Without a basement, we would not discover the staircase waiting in front of us. Without a basement, we would not let go of an outdated season. Without a basement, we would not embark on the difficult journey of discovering who we really are.

In this book, Apostle Kirby Gant shares his journey as a man who healed. He also offers raw and unpolished truth that will help you heal. This is not a fluffy book… this is a book for the warrior inside of you! This is a book that speaks to your highest form of masculinity and your greatest potential. This is a book that will arm you to live fully engaged in every moment and come out on top in spite of what the devil did. It is time to find the lesson in the basement and ascend the staircase of destiny and healthy masculinity.

Enjoy. Grow. Learn. Heal… and *become.*

I am proud of you, my kingdom brother.

Ryan LeStrange

Author of the Amazon #1 New Release ***Exposing Emotional Manipulation***

INTRODUCTION

I'm inspired to share with every man who's reading this book. Perhaps you're in an extremely difficult space, within your life, and due to the nature of your circumstances, you've been somewhat forced into silence... This book is for you.

The truth is that every man seeks a way out when he's lost in his troubles. We seek validation that affirms us positively. We need to know that the vocal support and physical presence from those who surround us are genuine.

A troubled man is a hurting man. Those times of uncertainty will often lead him into corners where he will perfectly fit and sit in.

Listen, Man. You have the power to stand in your pain. You have the ability to get up and walk out of spaces that provide "hurting comfort." And I'm here to be your mental coach, to motivate you to locate your new beginnings.

Guess what? It's all in the very place you're in now, The Basement. ROCKBOTTOM isn't designed to feel good, but it's definitely there to be the very thing you need to start all over again. FOUNDATION!

CHAPTER 1

"THE PLAN OF SUCCESSION"

The first phase of succession is conception. We're all created with purpose. One of my beloved scriptures comes to mind.

Jeremiah 29:11 (NIV)
"For I know the plans I have for you," declares the Lord, "plans to prosper you and not to harm you, plans to give you hope and a future."

Our lives are sealed by God's promises. What's riveting is knowing that God doesn't lie. He knows everything about us. It's written clearly.

I want to put a plug here and share this, it doesn't matter what we face, we are destined for greatness. God's greatness is not only written word, but it's also a generational code. Succession runs through our bloodlines!

As we embark upon the journey of living, we are without thought, preparing for unknown battles.

These battles are stressful. They rob us of momentum, time is either paralyzed, and we're hindered, or we are consumed by what we perceive as obstacles that are impossible to conquer.

I'm thinking back on September of 2024, when I had an encounter with God. August of the same year, I was led to take a sabbatical for the entire month of September. Shut away in my condo, Abba visited me and told me to take an inventory of my life, things, and people.

He began to say, "I want you to take inventory of your life. Those who surround you today won't surround you tomorrow. Things you have now, you won't have those things tomorrow." Then he shared with me that he was giving me a hard reset.

On September 28th, I began my journey. I had no clue what was ahead of me, but I knew I had the endurance to experience it and to see it through. The Father didn't talk to me until he was ready. I had to be in a mental state of sobriety.

September 26 and October 9 were dates of divine revelation. Southwest Florida was in the middle of a weather crisis. We were hit by two hurricanes on those dates.

Hurricanes are indeed a force of nature. They have the willpower to move things around, to completely dismantle structure and order.

I wasn't aware of my own two hurricanes that were gonna hit and hit extremely hard.

1. I lost personal relationships that were very dear to my heart. Relationships that were destined to be forever.
2. The church I pastored for almost 9 years fell as though a bomb was planted and then detonated. An intentional implosion.

As we all know, the aftermath of storms is often devastating. We stand before rubble and memories. However, there's a critical decision; we must choose to clean up the mess we're not necessarily responsible for.

And that's a major task. Men are often to blame for damage. It's because of the weight of the damage, the way things look. I often say, "Perception is everything." If we fail to gain clarity, we will always be misled.

Sorting through what's left and assessing what's salvaged, we spark new beginnings. We do so without first making the decision to do so.

That's a power move! Before it hits the brain to decide, your spirit has already made the decision for you to have a new beginning. Bro, it's been determined; you will succeed!

Succession has an in-depth process. Process never talks to you. But it shows up unannounced, and it interrupts your life and flow.

This interruption is divine. It's indicative of who you will become and where you're headed. Your next is your best. Your best is your future.

I must admit, PROCESS SUCKS! It hurts, it's confusing, it changes your life. All of what you've been accustomed to has come to an abrupt pause or an ending.

Pause and End, become ONE when relating to process. Pause has the ability to break your speed, causing you to slow it down. While the end is the finality of an era. But together the two mean a New Beginning.

As you champion the cause of the process, your eyes become open to a newfound reality. [mental thought] "This process has not come to break me down, but it has come to usher me into newness." Those plans are sacred and loaded with God's abundance!

You, yes you brother, the best part of your process is, it has patience that's unmatched. Your only obligation *is to be and to do!*

The journey of Succession will have lots of moments of wanting to quit. But when you discover your WHY, that's the moment you become a force. Unstoppable and full of value.

Every man will doubt himself. And it's okay. It's understandable. It's a part of the process. Perhaps you're fighting to stay alive AT THE MOMENT.

You need to know, with every breath you breathe, "you're still breathing" to continue forward. Your breathing is divine, you're breathing because you're winning, brother.

There's someone counting on you. You cannot stop. You say, "I feel trapped." ... Your mind has the power to break and shatter the glass ceiling. Listen, your only way out is up.

I must tell you, Brother, you're not average. You're above it.

Proverbs 23:7 tells us, "As a man thinketh in his heart, so is he" ...

Your inner thoughts, beliefs, and intentions are responsible for shaping and building you.

Take a minute and digest this: You're in a great space. You're being refined and defined. And it's for a greater cause, a powerful purpose!

CHAPTER 2

"PARALLEL NARRATIVES"

When I think of the word narrative, I think of truths, lies, and opinions. A mixture of all within context, concerning someone or something.

2025 was a year of HELL for me! After losing in my personal life and losing the church I pastored, I then lost just about everything I owned.

And to be honest, losing my possessions was a different type of hurt. Things I earned. Items I purchased. All were valuable, each piece meant something to me.

But what kept me standing instead of folding was my belief, "everything I had to sacrifice, I'll get it all back" ... my confession, my belief, and my leaning post.

My refusal became my persuasion to continue to move forward. In the midst of loss, mental pain, and undeniable shame, I made a conscious decision to stand tall, even through my tears!

My decision to do so seemed as if I was producing heat that was too hot for me to handle. My phone ringing all day at different times. I was being asked questions, and I realized I was defending myself due to lies that were quickly spreading. Not just in the community I live in, but also in my communities of influence, networks, business, and ministry.

Confronting my opposers that could never stand in the paint with me would've been a total waste of time. I remember clearly God dealing with my mind and heart, him instructing me to remain quiet during that season.

Here are 8 valuable lessons for you, my brother…

- Be intentional about your decision to be relational.
- Create healthy boundaries. That's the beginning of real love.
- Always know that identity is attached to purpose.
- Never lay down your morals to make someone comfortable. They will adjust, or they will exit.
- The opposite of rejection is affection. What you've been longing for is on the opposite side of disappointment!
- Protect your personal space. Failing to do so, you become susceptible to the unwanted.
- If you talk too much, it'll be hard to defend your character.
- A man who preserves his mouth protects his character.

I've learned while on my journey that every truth, lie, and narrative became parallel to my journey.

Parallel Narratives are weapons that form to be your destruction, but God is so strategic that he determines that they serve a greater purpose.

Hence, the reason silence is a must during certain seasons and transitions of your life. Silence isn't fear, it's in fact mental muscle. You're building a strength that you've never had. And this is why the pain of your process is intense.

When God allowed me to have a piece of clarity about my next step, I adjusted my posture. I intentionally smiled daily. He showed me it wasn't over for me, as my opposers thought.

My Council of Elders were on my right and left side. And the best part of that dynamic is that none of them know each other, as they all live in different cities and states. So, all of the counsel I received from each of them came hot and fresh off the press!

My brother, you're in a space of trying to determine who's who. Your trust in men and women has been leveled to zero. It's time that you seek counsel from someone you don't know, or perhaps from someone you know, but they're not connected on the side of the spectrum that has tried to tear you down and ruin your life.

The very thing I once spoke against became the very thing I needed most. Therapy. I decided to pursue therapy. It seemed as though the council of Elders had given all they were to give or had to give.

The therapist I had was a woman. Very prophetic. Also, a minister. So, I knew my time with her would hit different.

My greatest appreciation for having this therapist was the fact that she wasn't biased. She challenged those areas of my life that no one had ever confronted.

Her approach was indeed strategic. I recognized her approach, but I also trusted her because I knew I was safe with her. She addressed things I knew were true.

Due to me being safe with her, I gave her space to ask those hard questions, to speak to those areas of my life that were not accessible.

My therapist gave language to experiences I couldn't word. Because they were dark and painful.

She pointed out truths I only admitted to MYSELF. There hadn't been a conversation before. But she was able to speak to it because she was able to see it.

To sum up my sessions with her, I'll say this: she was the best voice that was assigned to my journey. I experienced every "he-motion," but I also healed. Whatever I wouldn't speak to before, I learned how to do so. With confidence and self-love.

Parallel Narratives are hard. Sometimes they feel as though they have punches that can and will knock you out. But even if they do, you can still stand and bounce back. Parallel Narratives are not sanctioned by God to be your demise.

I want to encourage you, brother. Stay the course. Every parallel narrative serves a divine purpose: to shift you from this dry place and into your place of promise.
It's full of hope and abundance.

Each day you wake up produces a new mentality. You have to believe within yourself that you can do whatever you set your mind to doing.

Depression, Suppression, and Oppression are vampires of your now and future. Too often, they attach themselves to people who are always whining and complaining about what they have going on.

While everyone will experience Life, here's what you must know: when those who surround you are insensitive to your journey and process, but they're always highlighting their moments to you, those are the people you must detach from.

They will box you in, make you focus on them, and cause you to abandon your journey and the process thereof.

I think as grown and mature men, we can certainly agree with this; Opinions are present often, but they don't have the right to re-route us. During the last year, I heard countless opinions.

My only objective during that season was to maintain my focus and follow those who were assigned to speak in my life.

Regardless of what I heard in the midst of my brokenness and pain, I had to accept the hard truth: an opinion only has weight when I create space. It's vital to maintain mental stability when you're faced with opposition.

Yes, opinions can be extremely insulting and also hurtful when you're in a low place.

You have to consider who's talking, where they are in their lives, and what they have going on. Then ask yourself the question, "Are They Qualified To Speak To My Situation"?

9 times out of 10, the answer is NO! This is how you determine whose voice is qualified and carries weight to speak in your life, during hard seasons...

- He whose testimony is parallel to your current reality.

- Whoever shows up does NOT have an interest in finding out details. They're genuinely concerned about your well-being.

- The help shows up in silence. They prefer to remain anonymous.

- Your boundaries of self-protection are not broken or dismissed.

- There's no agenda outside of your weakness, brokenness, or vulnerability.

- An olive branch is offered. Accountability and Resources.

Never become biased while you're in a rough season of life. There are some friends whose access should be limited. Not because you can't trust them, but it's because they may not be able to speak to where you are in life at that moment.

Keep those kinds of friends close enough to keep you laughing and on standby, ready to raise a 'lil hell on your behalf.

There are 3 kinds of friends you need when you're in a rough season of life.

- Watchman. The friend who's quiet, but their presence is visible and strong. They are assigned to watch on your behalf, ensuring your peace is uninterrupted, and you maintain mental sobriety. Their attitude is, "I Got You." Always.

- Spokesman. This friend is a great listener. He will allow you to express your feelings without casting judgment. Your feelings are safe with him. But this friend will hold you accountable, redirect you when it's necessary, and challenge your unhealthy spoken thoughts.

- Lineman. The friend who will stand on the front line for you. He protects you. He's equipped both physically and spiritually. Character, Reputation, and Name are the 3 focal points he's concerned about. The lineman is your defense; he clears the way to make sure you WIN!

My brother, although your struggle is real, it's not winning. You are! Get it in your mind. Create a daily devotion when you're in a tough season.

Your daily devotion is a formula for grit and strength.
It will ground you.

It's another form of mental and spiritual accountability. You want to make sure your daily devotion is comprised of.

- God's Word.
- Prayer Time.
- Journaling.
- Spoken Affirmations.
- Smile on Purpose.

Parallel Narratives that consist of Truths, Lies, and Opinions are all present to serve a solid purpose. I'm telling you, on the other side of your struggle is the finish line.

Do what you must to ensure you make it. One last thing, it has nothing to do with who will be at the finish line to congratulate you. Success sometimes is about you and you only. You are your greatest audience!

CHAPTER 3

MENTAL LIQUID

I'm a critical thinker. Often, I sit and get lost in my thoughts. I analyze important moments. I compartmentalize a certain order, as to how I'm going to produce movement.

Because I'm a visionary, I have to see my way out of what has come to cause chaos and perhaps unexpected change(s).

If I can be transparent for a moment here, let me share this: I don't like surprises. I have to know what's going on. Although I don't go looking for the bad or good, I will search matters through in my mind and spirit.

When I'm inclined, I then begin to prepare. I talk less. I shut away. This isn't a fear factor, but rather a way for me to counteract. I'm rarely short of words.

The latter part of 2024 was the beginning of 2025. Of course, I had no idea of how it would all play out, but due to what God revealed unto me, I was ready.

Certain things were happening that I chose NOT to confront or address. A lot of those things were blatant. If I weren't in a state of mental sobriety, I would've crashed out.

When January 2025 hit, I received a call from a very well-known Prophetic Voice. He told me these words.

"You came before me today. And the Lord told me to call you and share with you. Prepare yourself now.

Your life will shift. Please pay attention to March, April, May, June, and July. These will be very critical months. Before things get better, things will get worse. In July, you will then begin to turn the corner."

Those words never left me. I witnessed it all happen. They were horrible. Lots of talking, some truths indeed, but MOST were lies. Disgusting lies. Things were said that made me want to get absolutely physical.

But I remembered what God said to me back in September of 2024. Months prior. I also remembered what the Prophet said. So, I held my peace. I cried. I laughed. I was angry. Listen to me, I didn't agree with God telling me to "Be Quiet." All I thought of was fighting.

One year, I wasted time. I sat in silence. It was painful. Indeed, it caused me to become fragile. Although I was instructed to remain quiet, I wasn't instructed to lose focus. My passion for life itself slowly slipped away.

As each month passed, the pain increased. I was stuck in idle. I had a fear that developed from not knowing what was ahead. It seemed as though I was in a tunnel. Total darkness. Couldn't see (discern). I was the definition of an emotional wreck.

Halfway through 2025, I'm realizing it's time to pivot. I didn't have much strength, but I had a mind, and that critical thinker within me was triggered. I'm looking at what's left of my life, and I wanted to get up and do something that needed to be done, GET UP!

What's "Mental Liquid"?
The reality of your current state of mind and Life.

- Traumas
- Assessed Damages
- Faults
- Failures
- Losses
- Dead Ends
- Unbroken Cycles

I chose to kill excuses, self-pity, and the need for attention, which kept me sick emotionally. I took a look deep within and admitted that I had spent too much time grieving over people, matters, and losses that time had expired on. It was time to move forward.

Brother, the truth about new beginnings is taking accountability for your errors. You have to choose to allow whatever you've failed at to become building supplies for your new beginnings.

Those 7 factors mentioned above, I chose to use to build the life I'm destined to live. YOU SHOULD do it too!

Self-Investing is the best you can do for yourself when you're starting over, when seeking a resolution, and proving to yourself, "I can do this." You realize everything you need to do is already within you.

Brother, your mind is RICH! You've outlived the lies and established a new order by defying what was, or currently is, against you.

Mental Liquid is exactly what you need to rebuild your life, create a new stream of happiness, and thrive.

Listen! You were subdued, but you survived. You're the voice for many men who are waiting on you to show up!

CHAPTER 4
"THE DOPAMINE FACTOR"

Life has a way of altering certain dynamics. As we build, plan, and structure our lives, the truth is, we don't consider what lies ahead.

We're often captivated by tunnel vision, due to our commitment to stay focused on what's closely in view.
There are projects, deadlines, goals, inspirations, dreams, and visions that we have hope for.

Having all of those factors is great, but what's important is not being so caught up with the good that's happening, until you fail at discerning what's ahead, knowing who surrounds you, and hidden agendas.

It's true, people (some) will continue to smile and show support, all the while having a deep disdain against you. Such great pain and confusion enter the mind and heart when this type of thing occurs.

Before you read further, I challenge you to take a quick assessment of your life…

- Where are you in life at the moment?

Journaling

____

____

- How's your mental health?

Journaling

- Do you value YOU, in the midst of great loss and failures?

Journaling

- Do you believe in yourself NOW?

Journaling

- Have you allowed unresolved trauma to redefine you? If so, in what way(s)

Journaling

These questions are extremely vital to your now, tomorrow, and future. Take a minute to journal each answer on the pages that have been designated for this purpose.

Your answers will then become somewhat of a compass, as you consciously decide to journey forward!

Dopamine - the mental neurotransmitter that's responsible for the part of the brain that processes reward and reinforcement learning.

Brother, you're responsible for the decisions to improve your life, on every level. It's been proven that people do trigger certain emotions, but our happiness is left up to us.

When men are found in great shape, mentally, physically, emotionally, and spiritually, it's an automatic factor for us to smile.

An authentic smile is a smile whose owner has been through hell and has an understanding. PURPOSE is defined by my decision to live. To be well. To be whole.

One of the things that my therapist identified is that I'm known for smiling. It's true. But that was a powerful moment. Without realizing it, I began to smile.

What was spoken triggered my brain to process spoken language, and because it was true, an emotion was sparked like fireworks. The only thing I could think about during that moment was, "It feels so good to smile again."

Dopamine is a mental liquid! A literal substance God created. It matters NOT how bad things are. I wanna tell you, your smile is so powerful it will make you want to pick up the broken pieces of your life and begin the rebuilding process.

For seven months, I didn't have a genuine smile. It was forced. With each smile, I would incite a level of anger, because behind that smile were unhealthy thoughts. I had no idea of how deep I had fallen into depression, oppression, and suppression.

Depression - a mental disorder due to loss, grief, and emotional instability.

Suppression - a mental decision or voluntary choice to remain functional in unhealthy moments.

Oppression - a complex mental system sustained by one's belief, unchecked power, and unhealthy authority.

During my 8 1/2 years as Sr. Pastor of a thriving church, I wasn't aware of an unhealthy dynamic that was slowly killing the vision I worked so very hard for. I made sure things were happening.

I think back on my third session of therapy. My therapist told me that I taught everyone who surrounded me to be dysfunctional. She suggested, "Kirby, before you respond, think about it." I couldn't process that because it didn't sound right.

It was then said, "Because you don't like the word NO, you taught everyone who surrounded you to say yes."

They weren't necessarily "yes men/women," but they were people who loved you.

So, they always made sure to make certain things happen, even when they didn't agree. I must admit, when I processed what my therapist said, I accepted it. It was a hard truth.

A truth that challenged me to never again function without making space for my authority or power to be checked.

Here's the deal, brothers: what makes us great in our role as leaders within our spheres of influence is the necessity of being accountable.

When there's a lack of accountability, there's a lack of integrity. And this is why (low) dopamine produces unhealthy emotions.

Escaping the harsh truths of your character and emotions, you will also hinder yourself, of course, but you will also hinder those who are subordinate to you.

REFOCUS, RECALIBRATE, REBUILD

These words are vital for activating a new beginning.
You have no time for negative press.

- Critics that are negative AFTER you've lost and or failed, are abusers of your mental. Avoid them!

Dopamine recognizes your decision to pursue betterment. Catch this, your dopamine's way of communication is powerful.

Because men are visual, dopamine deals with our inner sight. We began to see those things that are important and substantial. And from there, we are able to gain back momentum, clarity, and hope.

High Dopamine vs Low Dopamine.

Let's sort through these 2 channels of the brain; self-discovery is always a turning point. Especially when it's done without biases, but rather with truth and transparency.

Here are two keys that I must mention.

- **Cognitive Function** - It influences executive functions, including memory, attention, and problem-solving.

- **Movement** - It plays a vital role in coordinating smooth, controlled body movements.

Trauma certainly plays a major role in the production of triggering low dopamine.

If we're not in a healthy state of mind, when it's time for decision-making, that will cause us to pivot positively, we fail, and we fall.

Before there's an outward expression of failure, there's mental failure first. There's no such thing as "overnight failure." Instead, a 3-step process.

- Situations
- Avoidance
- Kill-Switch

When situations arise that upset, cause breakdowns, and or even change particular dynamics, if we're consumed by the thoughts that don't offer solutions to fix situations, we then settle in sadness.

"A man that's lost in sadness, chooses to settle in pride."

Avoidance now becomes the compass that will lead and guide you into a reality that wasn't intended for you.

"A man who refuses truth, his life becomes a lie."

Being governed by emotions that low dopamine creates is what makes the man pull the "Kill Switch."

He can't see past failures because he's spent entirely too much time holding a magnifying glass, magnifying every mistake, every bad decision, and now he's prone to do nothing except fail.

Lean in for a moment... I'm not here to make you feel bad. I am here to be your "MC" - Mental Coach. I'm anointed to stimulate your spirit, strike a match in your mind, and awaken you.

1 Corinthians 16:13 (ESV)
Be watchful, stand firm in the faith, act like men, be strong.

I'm speaking to brothers who are reading this, and you've reached a dead end. It doesn't mean things are over.

NOT AT ALL!

But it means you're now being rerouted. Many of us had to experience routes that delayed timing, slowed down our process, and even caused us to go in different directions.

God is so gracious! He lets us know that he was there with us the entire time.

When we realize that we don't have to settle for an untimely end, and we choose to reroute our lives, the pursuit of a healthy life begins.

Now, we're starting to feel good within ourselves. Smiling was a thing of the past. It's now a current manifestation. Emotions are being regulated positively. Our dopamine levels are rising as each day goes by.

Your moods are climbing the healthy chart. Your movement is smooth. You have decided to live beyond sorrowful negativity. You're taking your life back. Purpose is being reestablished.

My brother. This is the activation of High Dopamine.
Failure isn't taboo. But it is a stepping stone that will help you cross over. Listen, you're on a newfound road of self-discovery, self-care, and self-love.

CHAPTER 5

"THE EFFECTS OF A BASEMENT"

Life happens to everyone. I'll even say this, "Life Be Life-ing." Ugh! Who lies down at night to rest their mind and body, just to wake up and have a day full of troubles!? NONE OF US!

We don't plan for failure. We don't prepare for unscheduled losses. We don't even look forward to our physical demise.

What we do and have always done, and that's, live decent lives. We find our paths in life. We discover the rhythm that coincides with our manly nature.

Here are 5 points of a Man's Nature

- Creative Abilities
- Career(s)
- Love Life
- Family
- Health

Every man has that passion for success. We will go great lengths just to make sure our future's success is locked and loaded.

We are aware that there will be challenges. Things come to break our focus. The determining factor of our outcome is deciding whether we will not allow anything or anyone, hinder or stop our progress.

I'm certain of God's word. When we are faced with life-altering moments, we have to counteract those moments with what His word says. Here's a scripture I love to recite, not because I'm faced with opposition, but because I find peace...

Romans 8:28 (NIV)
And we know that in all things God works for the good of those who love him, who have been called according to his purpose.

Read that again. Let it sink into your spirit and even into your psyche. That's a powerful and sure word that reminds us, EVERYTHING we face has a purpose. It must work out for our good.

Perhaps, you're in a season that's been tough. You've lost much. You've failed at some things. Maybe your family structure has been interrupted, and nothing looks promising.

I've gotta tell you, "IT'S WORKING." Something great will come out of this season of turmoil. Failure doesn't have to be forever. The decision is left solely up to you to decide.

When I hit ROCKBOTTOM and found myself in mental anguish, I experienced every emotion. After a year, I realized my life wasn't over. I then began to ask God for revelation: What am I to gain from all of this?

One of the greatest revelations I received was, "RockBottom Has A Basement." After it settled within my spirit, I pondered until I gained clarity.

God does his best work in the dark!
Although darkness became my reality, I determined it had to

work for me. In pain, in shame, embarrassed, and angry. God wasn't finished with me.

Each day spent in the basement, my refusal gained strength. I had made up my mind to develop a plan to exit. It wasn't about vengeance, but rather my recovery.

I ask God to show me everything I needed to see while being in the basement. He shone a light. As I began to look around, I saw written images. Failure, Caution, Hazard, all were boldly before me. My life and possessions appeared to be as debris.

Refusing to soak in grief and sadness and every other emotion, I looked up and behold, right before me, I read these words, "GET UP." From that moment, mental muscles were activated. God's word became as reverb…

*"**13** I can do all things through Christ who strengthens me".*
(Philippians 4:13)

It was loud and piercing in my ears and within my spirit. I then found myself standing straight up, chest out as a man should.

I am a man of prayer. But I must be honest, that season was difficult for me to pray as I normally would. But according to

Romans 8:26, the Holy Spirit prays for us.
"Likewise, the Spirit helps us in our weakness.
For we do not know what to pray for as we ought, but the Spirit himself intercedes for us with groanings too deep for words."

I want you to know this: when you can't find anyone else to stand in the gap for you and pray, the Holy Spirit will. There's a spiritual language that transcends our language, human reasoning, and logic.

What you cannot say, the Holy Spirit can and will. When you're in the dumps of life, the Holy Spirit is praying for you. And even now, prayers are being rendered unto God on your behalf. You're winning. Trust and believe it!

I'm now in a space in my mind and spirit. I'm ready to walk out of this basement. It was a temporary hold. I'm out now. As I continued on my journey, I then found myself having Self-arrangement. I'm arranging myself to take back self-authority and reinforcement learning.

This is what you, brother, have to do! You can no longer sit in that mental space; that's unhealthy. Please take heed to the fact that no one else wants to sit and or live with you in total darkness.

The basement became the place for me to recognize that my life wasn't over. I'm breathing because there's more life to live. You're there now. You're breathing. There's more life to be lived.

I hit RockBottom, and I hit it hard! I made a conscious decision to allow the basement to become the ground I used to stand upon, pivot, and walk out of.

Before I exited, I took a few mental notes. I'll share them below…

- Failure was truth. But failure wasn't in control.

- Hazardous indeed, because all around me were things that reminded me of what I had. But those very things became trash. I had to leave them there.

- Cautious. Pay close attention to ensure what you leave behind doesn't cause you to fall on your way out.

- The Door. Go ahead and walk out. No need to be ashamed of what you survived.

My brother, I encourage you to choose to live beyond the basement. For me, it became "The Foundation of All Things New." So shall it be for you!

CHAPTER 6

"HOW DID WE GET HERE"?

Things that make you go, hmmm. Right!?

My exact thought process during my time of decompressing. February 25th (this year), I had a moment.

This date is my sister's birthday, and after taking her out for breakfast, I returned home. I began thinking, "Wow. My first time being at Cracker Barrel in over a year."

It was triggering because it's not only a favorite place of mine to eat, but it was also a frequent visit between two individuals and me, who I was once very close to. Truth be told, I still love them. Dearly!

As I sat on my bed, memories flooded my mind. And I was thinking, my friendship of 8 years was over. Two people who meant more than the world to me.

Social Bonds are often forged over routines. And we had a weekly routine that we were very committed to. Mondays were our time together.

Lots of laughter, wholesome conversations, trash talking, moments of spirituality shared, and countless lessons.

One of the things I love doing is spending quality time. In fact, it's one of my love languages. I think time spent speaks in high volumes.

Time allows you and the other parties to establish a healthy dynamic of camaraderie. Although spending time at a restaurant isn't necessarily private, the moments are private.

Table talk equals Social intimacy. A dining room full of people, but not one single person there, can share in your moment.

"A Table For Three."

My mind functions differently, so follow me closely as I unravel this. Perhaps, it'll speak to you in some ways.

As I mentioned, Mondays were the normal routine between my two friends and me. I quickly learned the essence of what Mondays truly meant.

Indeed, it was a day off for me, aside from my normal days of ministerial duties. Pastoring and itinerant preaching.

It was my day to be with my friends. Aside from breakfast or brunch, I would do a little shopping. Our local mall was included. Dillard's is my favorite department store to purchase three particular brands.

Ralph Lauren, because I love Polo. Travel Smart for my slacks. Very comfortable to wear while ministering. Magnanni for my dress shoes.

My friends knew that I did NOT have the capacity to walk through the mall. Being around too many people is something I despise.

One of the things I admired about them is that they allowed me to have my day. They both understood how important Mondays were to me.

In particular, my time in Dillard's. One of them certainly didn't give great advice on my choice of Polo. I'd ask her if she liked this or that. Her answer would always be, NO!

Now, it was established quickly that I could NOT hang with them when their time of shopping or mall browsing came around. I tried it with them a few times. Let's just say, I made them miserable.

So, moving forward, their time was girl time and not "friend time" as in the 3 of us. I was so impatient and inconsiderate. I definitely lacked compassion lol.

I repeat to you, this was 8 years of a routine. Some of my best times were shared with those two individuals.

A dining table has so much that it comes along with it. And it's beyond the facts of setting the table, but moreover, as in what the table allows you to establish.

Here are 5 true facts about the dining table.

Strength - it has the capacity to hold weight. Everyone uses the dining table to lean on.

Silence - table talk is a real thing! There are many conversations held while sitting at a table. And if you think about it, when it's time to leave, we tend to end conversations there.

Trust - whoever comes next to sit at the same table is unaware of what was discussed. The table is the bearer of confidentiality.

Longevity - we can agree to this fact; The table is what undergirds you and those that accompany you. Often, hours pass by, and dinner is finished. But we choose to continue to linger.

Emotions Experience Exchange - "The Triple E." If any one of the three doesn't bear witness to you, perhaps there's cognitive dissonance. It's proven that the table will awaken every emotion. Those emotions become an experience that leads to an exchange.

The table has a divine purpose. And that's to give space for whatever is needed. The table is the foundation of every true friendship. Why? Because the table is relational!

The friendship between my two friends and me wasn't established because I pastored them, and they were key leaders. Elders, to be exact.

Pastoring was the triggering factor that sparked the interest. I broke the ice and extended the invite for lunch. The food was good, but the time spent was even better.

We got to know each other. In every way. Many days and many hours produced a lifetime of great memories. The dynamics have now changed.

Those two are best friends. Although my ending with them was sour and will always be.

It will never take away from the fact that they were some amazing friends.

And for all that I was able to gain, I'll always cherish what we once had and shared as a trio. There's not enough disdain that could ever force me to downplay who they were to me.

"The Power of Social Bonding."

I believe that many do not know what it really means to say, "we have a bond." That word bond has 8 definitions, and I want to share some.

I'm getting ready to end this chapter, but I have to make sure you get exactly what it is I'm conveying to you!

Relationship Bond - A strong emotional connection, tie, or feeling of friendship between people.
I strongly believe there are levels to bonding. And here's my hypothesis. Please oblige me...

The above-mentioned, Relational Bond. It's basic. Primitive. Very easy to accomplish. In most cases, being friendly is all it takes to incite friendships. But friendships have levels, too.

You can have a friend or two, but be very guarded. And it's natural. There's a distance you allow yourself to go when the friendship is basic.

However, there's a bond entitled Social Bond. I must admit, it sounds simple. But it's not. Social Bonding has four power points.

May I share them? Cool. Thank you for saying, "Sure."

Attachments - the connecting emotional ties between friends.

Commitment - the investment in the relationship, as well as the bond.

Involvement - the agreeable participation; presence, as in showing up. Equal Accountability.

Belief - a mutual exchange between friends. "I believe in you. You believe in me." A commonality of morals.

Without 4 power points, it's impossible to prove Social Bonding. There's always proof in the pudding— it's not about what you say, but what you do!

You may be curious about wanting to know what happened with my friendship of 8 years, I had with those two individuals.

Well, I'll share this. When you have established a friendship, social bonding is a genuine part of what's shared.

The truth is, you have to be careful about whom you may allow to access what you and your friend(s) have worked so hard to build.

It's okay to have as many friends as you desire. But it's vital to know clearly, who's who and what's what!
Please, don't ever be afraid to classify.

Relationship Bonding is for basic friends only.
Social Bonding is strictly for best friend(s).

There's such a thing as people not being happy for you when they see you being happy and even at your best.

I've learned over the years that Social Bonds don't necessarily mean that there's an equal commonality when it comes to strength.

You can be the strongest, and the other friend(s) may not be as strong as you are. That's perfectly fine.

Now, is it important to be strong? Yes. Very much so. And I get it, there are times when our strength will not be up to par. Hence, the reason communicating is imperative.

This is where accountability has its role. Social Bonds (should) prove loyalty when it's time. When someone who's NOT invested, but rather simply basic, has an accusation against who you're bonded with, you are to let it be known, "listen, I will be letting my friend know all of what you said, and I will share your name."

And this is what happened within my friendship. I was accused of a few things. One of my friends and I had lunch one day. That's when I found out that I was being blamed for some things I did not say or do.

I was taken aback. I am very confrontational. Verbally and physically. So, speaking my mind has never been a struggle. I'm going to tell you exactly how I feel.

While listening to my friend share the accusations, I asked her, "Who's this person"? She refused to tell me.

It was that moment I said, "Since you won't tell me, this is no longer my problem. It's yours. You deal with it."

Walking away from that toxic moment was only the beginning of an ending I didn't see or expect. Lies on top of lies is what ultimately destroyed my friendship.

My stance was, "I'm a grown man. Whatsoever I say once, I will say 3 times". I was able to take that stance and not worry about anyone checking me. I wasn't going for it. It was and still is the TRUTH!

Brothers, I wanna say to you, don't ever dumb down to narratives about you that aren't the truth. You have a right to speak up for yourself.

"Lies Have Speed, But Truth has Endurance"

As you navigate through the turmoil of losing relationships you truly invested in, your decision to move forward is a healthy move. But you must move forward in peace and with acceptance.

Although I miss my friends and all of the years we shared together, I gotta tell ya— I CHOOSE ME. Nothing or nobody is worth me losing myself in the process of an existing transition.

I challenge you, brothers. Do an inventory of your relationships. What needs to be pruned, you must take action and get to pruning.

"Procrastination Fears Tomorrow.

CHAPTER 7

"RESHAPE, REFRAME, REBUILD"

These are the stepping stones to ensure you become a healthier version of yourself.

My mental process is definitely different. Some of my greatest friendships have always been with the opposite sex.
Perhaps it's because of my family structure and dynamic, while being raised. My biological father was present, but he was more likened unto a "visible ghost." Literally.

And this isn't shade towards my father at all. I 200% admire, honor, and respect him with every fiber of my being.

My mother was the disciplinarian. She was there for us in every way. Dad was a street man. He provided. Looking back, his greatest provision for his family was security. In the midst of growing up in the "Projects," he made sure we were safe!
My mother raised 3 daughters, and I'm the only son. My grandmother also had a major role in my upbringing. She's responsible for my spirituality as well. She was a singer and a praying woman!

I wanted to be just like her. The singer was in particular. If anybody could mimic her sound, it was me. I took pride in that. My grandma was a powerful singer.

My father's side of the family was closely knit. I remember they all lived within close proximity of each other. Neighbors. Literally.

Auntie Tricia was the glue that held the Gant Family together. She was my father's eldest sibling. She wasn't the matriarch during her time, but she led the family pack.

Yes, there were strong men in my family dynamic. Both sides had the presence of men. My mother has 5 brothers. All of whom are great men, husbands, and fathers.

My father has a brother. And my first male cousins were much older than I was. They were military men. Then there were the older Uncles. Having a ton of male cousins. All of us were athletes and fighters. I'm sharing these facts to let it be known that my life as a male child growing up was exceptional.

Having more influence by the women of my family wasn't because there was a lack of presence from my father or any other male factor.

Mama, Grandma, and Auntie were my greatest influences. That's the way God designed it. Today I am thankful. I have NO regrets.

My sisters are my heartbeats. Everyone knows how I feel about my sisters. So, having female friends or best friends is what I choose. It works for me.

Do I have male friends? Absolutely. Two of my very best friends are men. One of almost 40 years. The other 30 years. Both solid men with their own families.

Social Bonding for me is vast. Many asked sometimes, how do you have so many best friends?

My response has always remained the same. Balance is everything. What works for me may not work for you. I'm a high-functioning, spiritually gifted, intelligent man. I am what each of my best friends needs me to be for them. And they are what I need.

How does it work, you may ask?

Well, the best part of my Social Bonds is that I don't collide any of the friendships together. None of them are the same. I sense that while writing this chapter, there would be a brother or two (maybe you) who can relate to this particular chapter.

Life transitions can cause us to have moments reflecting on family and friendship dynamics. Sometimes it's because of the unhealthy minds of men and women that surround us. When relational situations happen, some will try to gauge you from their low-level perspectives, which are off and absolutely have nothing to do with what's current in your life.

The bottom line is this: you're going through life. Relational Bonds and Social Bonds aren't promised to be forever. We have to produce the fruits of longevity for as long as THAT tree of longevity is destined to live. PERIOD!

During the process of pruning your life, please don't do so without carefulness. Reshaping, Reframing, Rebuilding.

Reshaping speaks to the new blueprint of what you desire life to be for you.

Reframing is the process of renewing your mind and your character.

Rebuilding is the power to move forward after life as you once knew it fell apart and crumbled to nothing.

I'll leave you with this to think on…

2 Corinthians 5:17: "Therefore, if anyone is in Christ, he is a new creation. The old has passed away; behold, the new has come".

My brother, God's word is truth and sure. Trust him, believe him, follow him!

CHAPTER 8

"A FEW GOOD MEN"

Life has a way of bridging divine purposes together. When I think of my life, my younger years in ministry, and my development, I can't help but think of my extended brothers.

My younger years as a teenager were quite interesting. I've always been a jovial type of person. Laughing was something I did intentionally.

At the age of 15, I joined an all-male singing group called "PNW". A group of young men who were in their mid-teens, and then three who were in their early 20's.

The older brothers were either engaged or married. Their partners were singers. Aside from the all-male chorus, there was another singing group called "EOP." Ensemble of Praise. Both young men and women.

We were literally family. Singing is what we were known for, but having solid relationships with Christ is what we ultimately strived to produce. We aimed to live godly lives.

Our coming together weekly wasn't just rehearsals, but times of corporate prayer and fasting as well as Bible study. In my opinion, we were a "floating church." We were virtual before virtual actually became an active mechanism.

I can think back on our years of traveling to minister songs in concerts, conferences, and revivals. The main focal point for any occasion was soul-saving!

Here we are, 30-plus years later, and we are all still brothers. All of us have our own families. Each of us has experienced life in whatever way(s) it presented itself to us.

Singers, Musicians, Preachers, Pastors. We were being raised to be who we are today. There were many lessons taught and learned over the years we spent as a singing ministry. Many core values I still govern myself by today.

Life today. The experiences, the connections, the friendships, the opportunities are nothing like they were 30 years ago. I'm aware of the fact that we all evolve. Progression is a choice every person chooses to make.

However, digression is due to refusing to change. Bad behaviors, piss poor character, no integrity, the lack of accountability, and denial of self-awareness; Getting older is mandatory, but growing up is optional.

Parenting, Morals, Values, Family, Villages, and Community have vital roles in who we are destined to be.

Within the Structure of Black Communities (when I was being raised), our Villages consisted of those figures who weren't biological family members.

We had Uncles and Aunties that were not related by blood but related by way of Social Bonds. In some cases, our older saintly neighbors had a hand in with us.

The "Mr. & Misses, So & So's" watched out for us. They would correct us when our behaviors were out of the norm. Often letting us know, "I'm gonna tell ya, daddy and mama."

It was a network that couldn't be denied. Nothing was a secret. Everybody knew everybody, and just about every other person was related to you or someone else who knew your family.

Take a moment and reflect back on your upbringing. We may not share identical stories, but I bet in some kind of way our stories are parallel.

"The Power of Foundation."

When I think of foundation, many things come to mind. When I look around me, and I see that I still have those brothers from 30 years ago, still active in my life, I can't help but realize it has everything to do with our foundation.

Foundations that we were able to construct and build on top of, because of how we were raised. That's where it all begins.

"Yesterday Shapes Your Tomorrow."

Brothers, the fruits of your life are determined in three ways.

Below are the 7 fruits of the Family.

- Family Blueprint
- Family Building
- Family Morals
- Family Traditions
- Family Beliefs
- Family Values
- Family Support

These fruits are always determined by Generational transference, Parental activation, and Self continuation.

In each, there's the power of me. When you reach adulthood, you consciously decide if you're going to continue to carry on, what has been a strong erection, or to rewrite the narrative.

Some people do great at carrying on what has been laid out for them. But some fail. Failing isn't always a bad thing. Divine purpose can often be discovered in failure.

We have all failed at something. Lord knows I've had my share of failing. But it has been my fighting nature that has made me stand up every single time to get me back in the ring with this thing called LIFE!

Brothers, don't ever be afraid to establish that strong connection with just A Few Good Men.

It's so necessary to do so. Trust me on this one. I'm writing this manifesto because I've lived it. Every part of what you've read thus far and will continue to read til the end.

I'm surrounded by some great and powerful brothers and friends. Some of those friends are strong women.

I want to highlight the brothers and friends I've deemed as **"My Riders."**

I won't mention names, but when they read the book, they will know who they are...

- My vocal coach
- Island Boy
- Janky Jubilee
- The Bee
- Knuck Buck Nation
- Sweet Practitioner
- Creole Sensation
- Shotgun Betty

You gotta have those friends that you know, that will allow you to rest while they watch for you. They've gotta be the same friends that don't mind getting in the mud with you.

These are the same friends who will raise hell with you and for you. They're quiet in their own way. But don't get it twisted, their silence isn't to be mistaken.

The 8 mentioned are living exceptional lives, but hear me, they will wrestle you about me.

Bro! You owe it to yourself to build that type of rapport with your riders. You can't be a punk (scary), and all of your riders are fighters.

If the time should ever come and they need reinforcement, you have to be the one or the 3 they choose to call, and you show up. Boots on the ground, ready to kick up some dust!

Without question or doubt, I have that in my riders. They were actively present during the entire year of 2025. They shared in my pain.

They gave language to what was too hard for me to convey. They understood me. Allowed me to be who I was. Most importantly, they were the voices I heard from during that rough season. Just about every day.

Within those 8 people, I knew I could trust them with every part of me. They've never given me a reason not to trust them.

When I sit and think of each of them, aside from the nicknames I gave them, there are words that describe them. Each word is what they represented during all of 2025.

Let's take a look below.

— responsibility
— discipline
— vision
— standard
— pressure produces
— conflict resolutions
— accountability
— focus

Listen to me, we all need those individuals who represent what we need. They are modeling examples.

Not just for us to get lost in awe, but to take notes and ensure we embrace the instructions, challenges, and insights that they share. It's for our good!

When you've gone through hard seasons, redefining moments, and divine resets, some people are already present in our lives, and God will amplify their presence and purpose. "The Why" they are here becomes an undeniable revelation.

You may have countless people who love you, and it's great to know it as well. But I'm telling you, it's only a few that will stand with you and get low with you, during those seasons you need them the most.

A Few Good Men were created and chosen by God for you. You simply accepted them. Now, do what you must do to protect them, honor them, respect them, and love them.

"WE RIDE AT DAWN."

CHAPTER 9
"TRIGGERS & TRIUMPHS"

Let's breathe, stretch, and shake!

Triggers. When I think of triggers, I think of many. What's interesting is that I've never used the word or paid any attention to its meaning until the latter part of 2024.

Trigger - a stimulus that causes a quick reaction. An activating mechanism. A cause that incites strong emotional and often traumatic responses.

Triggers don't necessarily always have to be bad. There are good triggers. And the truth is, we all have triggers.

Now, depending upon what someone has experienced, the word (trigger) itself can send that person on a downward spiral, causing a mental decline.

That explains many behaviors we've witnessed or even heard of. I have to be honest and share that I was that person. The thought of the word made me think back on certain devastating moments from 2025.

I've shared with you how I went through therapy. But therapy didn't teach me how to compartmentalize my mind and or responsive language, when it came to particular words.

Please understand, my therapist was great and divinely appointed. Therapy is a guiding tool. However, I believe there are certain matters that we have to consciously decide to become adequate enough to deal with.

Hearing the name of a certain individual always triggered me into anger. And when I took the initiative to deal with that part of me, I realized I hadn't done what was vital. It was a loss I didn't grieve properly.

I was stuck. Frozen in place. One day, it was like a light that turned on. And then revelation was given.

Why are you triggered over a matter and an individual who owes you nothing? A decision to process through this quickly is the final resolve!

I sat and pondered my thoughts thoroughly. And BOOM, clarity was given. There's a need for "Mature Conscious Awakening."

Mature Conscious Awakening. The nature of embracing your higher self. This is being in a place of mental sobriety.

Your readiness has fruit to prove it. Your methods aren't low vibrational, and there isn't any need for self-gratification!

It takes hard inner work to get to this space. You can't pretend to be in this realm or state of mind. It'll show you up every single time.

I'll share some signs of "MCA." Mature Conscious Awakening.

- **Heightened Self Awareness.** You're more locked in with yourself, behaviors, choices, and certain patterns. You have a deeper knowing and or sense to align yourself properly.

- **Inner Peace & Authenticity.** Unhealthy habits, unproductive connections, low vibrational relationships, constant carnal conversations & the need to prove yourself— have all expired. You seek peace. You develop a sense of inner-self-renewal. You have a newfound attraction towards nature!

- **Physical & Emotional Alignment.** As you mature and accept there's a "higher you," you're aware more so now than ever before that there's a need for change. These changes often start within the mind. They'll spill over into your emotional state. Mental improvement is vital to you now. And the craving to physically evolve. Your focus is on eating properly and doing bodily exercise.

Mature Conscious Awakening isn't for the faint of heart. It's a journey, and it's likened unto a very intense course.

One of the signs of your awakening is the important need to face and conquer unresolved trauma.

What leads you to this space are your thoughts, which you seemingly can't avoid. Whether it's morning, high noon, or bedtime. It doesn't matter. It's there.

Unresolved trauma should have an expiration date. After it has ravaged your mind and spirit, you become numb to it. After a while, the effects it once had no longer work.

When realization grabs hold of your psyche, that's when you now process "THE HOW."

How am I going to approach this?

I wonder if there's someone I can talk to.

Can I really trust anyone?

Now that you're in your thoughts, you then begin to process whatever it was you experienced. And it's at that point you decide to pursue or maintain being still.

Depending upon where you are in your mind, it will also determine your strength to exercise your right of self-authority.

What's self-authority!?

The power of commanding your voice and physical movement. You've surpassed unwanted feelings of those invalid vulnerabilities. You've counted up the cost and fear no longer controls you.

One of the biggest reasons some men won't vocally share the stories of their trauma is due to those feelings of shame and embarrassment. Ultimately, we attach our trauma(s) to our EGO!

When you're void of inner healing, you're certainly full of pride. Pride muzzles the heart. A muzzled heart prevents the mouth from being vocally transparent.

It's impossible to CRY OUT for help, and when help shows up, the help can't help you. It's oxymoronic. Please, let's avoid that. It's past time!

There are types of trauma. But I'd like to deal with those traumas that are often found within MEN.

And here's the thing: these types of traumas are colorblind. They only see a boy, a teenage boy, a young man, a full-grown man.

Help Me Identify My Trauma(s)

- **Foundational trauma.** Where it all begins. But the truth is, foundational trauma has fruit that comes along with it.

- **Developmental/Early Childhood.** This speaks to what often happens in the womb: rejection. Abandonment is the second part. When the child is separated from the maternal and paternal order. If this type of trauma isn't addressed, it often leads to unpredictable behaviors, lifestyles, and emotional instability.

- **Systematic Trauma(s).** This is a very common trauma. It isn't rare at all. It affects men from every culture and or walks of life.

- Causes by institutions such as prisons, jails, and rehab centers. Societal Structures such as racism and poverty.

Cycles of trauma are born when there aren't proper and healthy formats to confront and deal with the effects that come along as a result of being institutionalized.

- **Intergenerational/Historical Trauma(s).** Traumas that travel through generational bloodlines. One of the biggest of these: failure without hopes of restoration and recovery. This type of trauma surrounds talented men, particularly in the area of sports. Once, an outstanding athlete such as the fathers and mothers were. Then it's those talks that are heard... "Athletes run in the family, but none of them reached that pinnacle of success." WHY!?

We can all attest to knowing one or several men who have this background. Some are on the streets. Some are drug addicts. And some are just living life. And it's all due to the truth; they couldn't bypass what was established. Failure. Now, all you hear is, "they were a great athlete."

Intergenerational trauma(s) doesn't just begin or end with sports and the talented man. That's just one fact mentioned.

Cumulative emotional injury. It's real. This injury can be caused by many things, but when it's generational, it's usually attached to the same experience. Failing to seek healthy help, which provokes inner healing, will only keep you in the same state of existing.

Existing with your trauma!

- **Physical Abuse/Sexual Abuse.**

A hard area to tackle. Many men today who have faced these two types of trauma aren't just men who are attracted to the opposite sex. That's low-level thinking.

There are men whose sexual preference is rooted in curiosity, early introduction based upon what they found in mama and daddy's closet. Explicit videotapes and magazines. The other introduction comes from an older cousin, uncle, and or the sneaky male friend, who runs-a-muck in the neighborhood.

Some men who choose to indulge in sexual encounters with women and aren't quite satisfied— they tend to experience the same sex. You think it's taboo. It's not. And believe me, those same men aren't effeminate. They're masculine, hardcore, and tough.

The percentile rate is 35%. That's very high considering the fact that man was created to lie with the woman. That's God's nature and law. Anything outside of that is by choice!

Allow me to list these 10 triggers and struggles.

- **Abuse**
- **Sexual Addictions**
- **Unhealthy habits**
- **Gambling**
- **Drugs**
- **Alcohol**
- **Rejection**
- **Abandonment**

- **Insecurities**
- **Failures**

The reason I mentioned these 10 triggers is to point out what real life is. There's a brother reading, and he's been able to identify his area(s) of truth.

This isn't judgment, this is revelation. My greatest desire in writing this book is to provoke permanent transformation, from the inside out!

"SEX & PHYSICAL ABUSE" cont'd...

Sexual encounters with lots of women, and still, there isn't satisfaction, that's perverted passion. It's proven!

It's not about the same-sex or opposite sex attraction. It's now more so about an appetite that's uncontrollable and makes you live a secret life of mental misery.

Deep down within, your soul is in anguish. You're seeking something you can't put language to, because all you've known is to make your "friendly part" happy.
Physical abuse is the same. Wait a minute. Men can be abused physically!? Absolutely. It's happening every day. Perhaps even while you're reading this.

Physical abuse starts when you're younger. But here's the flip side of THAT trauma: You're a grown man now, and you've never healed from childhood physical abuse. You're now the abuser.

You're cringing at the sexual piece. I know. But it's real brother. Don't get stuck there. I'm not accusing you, but I am stating truthful facts.

You may say, "I've had lots of women. I ain't never been with a man." That's great. But having multiple women as sexual partners doesn't prove your manhood. But it definitely speaks to a few things. One being "psychological immaturity."

Back to my address on physical abuse. What you don't correct will only mislead you. This area of trauma carries unmatched pride and deep inner shame. No man is pleased with himself for being any type of abuser.

These traumas have gone overlooked for years. Most of them are hard to confront because the men who wrestle with these two types are very aggressive and guarded. They don't hide their facial expressions, and they're not easily approachable.

GRACED TO TRIUMPH!

Brother, your greatest TRIUMPH is knowing that you can overcome any and all traumas. PERIOD!

It doesn't matter how long you've been fighting your traumas. What matters most is that you know what you're dealing with and are now in heavy pursuit of defeating the very things that have you bound. Trapped mentally. Trapped sexually. Trapped between bondage and freedom.

Identifying your struggle is easy. God created us to know and feel when something is wrong. Knowing what's wrong and what's right is a factor of biology.

Some of what we're taught comes by way of our inner man. Intuition. Discernment.

I have to tell my brothers, your triggers don't define you. I want you to know you're Triumphant. Life has a way of showing up and showing out, in negative ways. However, we have the power to be, to do, or the exact opposite.

What's a Triumph?

A triumph is a great victory, significant success, or the joy resulting from such achievement.

Pause for a moment. Read the above again. Let it get down in your spirit. Whatever your triggers are, you can overcome them. It doesn't matter how long it's been.

I can see the fighter in every brother reading this book. And I want to tell you, while you're on this journey of self and spiritual renewal, don't avoid the process. Stay in the fight until you've secured your victory!

5 Steps to Triumph

- **Identify (the problem)**
- **Healthy confrontation**
- **Remove every obstacle**
- **Vision & Blueprint for a reset**
- **Move forward in confidence**

2 Corinthians 2:14
Now thanks be unto God, which always causeth us to triumph in Christ, and maketh manifest the savour of his knowledge by us in every place.

As I end this chapter, I whisper this prayer for you, my brother…

"Father, I thank you for my dear brother who's on a journey of self and spiritual renewal. I pray for continuous clarity as they seek to conquer every trigger. I thank you in advance for the victory that is their portion. Triumphant is the man who places his life and trust in Christ. Amen."

CHAPTER 10

"I HAD A JUNIPER TREE"

As I continued on my journey, going through the process of self and spiritual renewal, I had to settle my mind.

Reality was starting to settle. I was approximately 60 days in, and my mental progress was between 0-1. I was completely depleted.

Sitting home during the week, I believe it was a Monday morning. One of my best brothers gave me a call around 10:30am.

"Rev., what's up, bro?" I'm trying to focus and mustard up the right words to say; "Chillin bro" ... Silence was blazing strong on the other end of the phone.

My bro circled the block, it seemed, and hit me with, "What you got going on, bro... listen, you need to get up and do something productive. Go stand outside on the balcony. Go sit by the pool" ...

Less than 120 secs, bro literally had given me 3 options to choose from. I had to pick one. Before the call went further, it felt as though he had driven around the block again, only to come back with more.

He gathered my entire frame of mind. Dismantled my thoughts. He put Jesus on me. It felt like a whooping— the kind your mama gives ya when you decide to show your behind!

What was ironic is this: I hadn't had one single opportunity to share anything that was going on. He only knew about the transition of the church. Our move from the hotel to an actual church building.

I'm puzzled. Blown away because I'm wondering who this dude talks to!? I knew from that moment, bro had a direct connection with the almighty God!

After I got myself together and avoided the unmerited need to be offended, I opened myself to my brother. I then took him down the rabbit hole and told him every single thing that had already taken place. From the start to the present point. He learned it all that day.

Now, before any manifestation of a transition or turmoil, bro and I were already talking daily. The year prior, I was able to partake in something that would change his life and ministry forever. I had promised him, "Bro. I'm here. I'm gonna walk you through this until the end." And that I did. With great pride and joy!

Only God knew what was coming down the pipeline for Kirby. And when it all showed up, piece by piece, my brother showed up. He showed up with presence and authority. He said to me, "Man, listen. You're gonna be fine. You will go through this process. You're going to finish and finish strong. I will be here every step of the way, just as you were there for me."

Since the latter part of 2024, up until now, my bro has been visible. He's been the voice of counsel and the ear to listen without harsh judgment.

There were moments I'd "cuss" the entire length and width of Interstate I-75. Sometimes he would laugh, and I did too. But there were those times he'd remain quiet. And after my rants were over, he would say, "You done.... Well, alright, you need to get some rest. Go lie down."

Being able to compartmentalize my thoughts and knowing how to carefully structure whatever I process through, I'm able to identify the divine purpose my brother served.

Let's take a look at the Juniper Tree. You know the very famous tree found in the Bible.

1 Kings 19:4-5
But he himself went a day's journey into the wilderness and came and sat down under a juniper tree: and he requested for himself that he might die; and said, It is enough; now, O Lord, take away my life; for I am not better than my fathers.

And as he lay and slept under a juniper tree, behold, then an angel touched him, and said unto him, Arise and eat.

The Juniper Tree is described as the source of 12 things. I'll deal with 6, which will bring us further into my points, that's going to pull all of it together here in this chapter. Continue reading...

This tree, which I've always been intrigued by, is significant because of what it represents.

Characteristics of a Juniper Tree

Big
Full
Fruity
Shady
Longevity
Protection
Purity
Recovery
Healing
Withstand
Structured
Covering

Last year, I was given a Juniper Tree by particular individuals. They each represented what I needed for my daily navigation. As much as I wanted to give up, I wasn't allowed to. God surrounded me!

Being that I've talked about my best brother, he represented "withstand." It was because of him that I didn't buckle at the knees and fall. He gave language that served as spiritual calisthenics.

Calisthenics - a form of resistance training using only body weight. This type of training is for overall bodily exercise and health!

James 4:7
Submit yourselves therefore to God. Resist the devil, and he will flee from you.

As I submitted unto God through my process and whom he chose to guide me, I learned the power of resistance. Physical exercise is painful because it stretches your body/muscles out of complacency. Growth is provoked. You can't expect a new type of you without first putting in the work.

My best bro was there every day. He challenged me beyond every expression I gave, which was a contradiction to my purpose.

Brothers, listen up. When you're transitioning from one space in life to another one, precisely pinpoint who shows up and stays til the end.

Every part of them is focused on you. They're not present to take anything from you. But rather, they are there to make sure you get whatever it is that you need to make it and become a greater version of yourself!

Withstand I did. And I proudly say it with all of my chest out. It was hard as hell, but I stood. Through mental anguish, brokenhearted, anger, suicidal thoughts, thoughts to inflict physical pain on one person in particular.

I was ready for whoever would've come running to their rescue. I had a plan. Prepared to take them out, one by one.

Best Brother had a connection with God that was mind-blowing. He would call during those moments, and he would say, "Bro, you will not self-destruct. Not on my watch. I'm not gonna let you. Find something else to do."

He would call me. I didn't call to tell him anything. I pretty much lived alone in my condo. One of my daughters was basically in and out. So, she would be gone most of the time.

Those phone calls were always on time. I'd answer and just listen. He would shift my focus.

I sense very strongly in my spirit to tell you, my brothers, you will make it. The adversary of your life doesn't have permission to make you abort your life's purpose.

Pray This Prayer

"In Jesus name, I bind and cancel the spirit of self-sabotage. Every foul-mouthed spirit that's tormenting me, I declare they're silenced, in Jesus name.

I come against self-destruction, I cancel defeat, I veto the untimely demise of my destiny and my life. In Jesus name."

Quote & Highlight This Scripture

Isaiah 54:17
No weapon that is formed against thee shall prosper; and every tongue that shall rise against thee in judgment thou shalt condemn. This is the heritage of the servants of the Lord, and their righteousness is of me, saith the Lord.

Pressing forward. My mind is slowly releasing those thoughts of mental pain and aggravation.
You're halfway through this chapter...

The voice of one of my greatest friends to ever exist. She's been present for 12 years strong. We've walked each other through some hard times. What I love about this friend is that she has never wavered.

She's been my rock, confident, my go-to for everything, and certainly that friend I trust with my life. Lord knows I've worked her nerves. We've even had our share of knockdowns and drag-outs.

Through all of what we've encountered, she's remained on all 10 of her toes. She's probably one of the strongest individuals I personally know.

Relating to The Juniper Tree, she's the part that provides "covering." She embodies the word in full totality.

Let me interject this right here: Brothers, it's imperative to have at least one person, a friend, who will stand with you through the crisis of life, to serve as your covering. Let's be honest, we all need somebody who's built to provide coverage!

Covering - substance used as layers to provide protection, to place on top of, to hide, and to conceal for the purpose of preserving...

Open your mind and spirit, and let me minister to you right here for a moment.

Elijah ran and hid underneath the Juniper Tree. He was running from Jezebel. I strongly believe he wasn't afraid of her. But rather, he was exhausted. He didn't have adequate help.

He needed a place to rest and rebuild himself. The scripture points out how the Angel gave him bread and water. Twice.

As bad as I needed The Juniper Tree, I was trying to avoid it. I wasn't running from nothing or nobody.

Elijah crashed out. I was trying to crash out too. I wanted to so bad. But that tree… I need to pause for a moment and say, Thank You, Lord, For That Tree!

Brothers, you're reading this right now, and your mind is reflecting back on certain moments. Life was truly life-ing, and you were on the verge of throwing away your destiny.

God stepped in and made you have a seat in a space that was out of your norm. But it was what you needed.

He put a voice in your life that wouldn't be afraid to speak to those flawed areas surrounding your character.

That same voice challenged your integrity. That same voice spoke to your potential because it had insight into your future. Their words became seed for sowing into your spirit.

Those seeds took root. God is strategic. He knew your growth process had to be different. So, he gave you a COVERING that would layer you and not expose you!!!

I sat under that tree, and I had the right one serving as my covering. She didn't relent because of my attitude. She had one too. Maybe three!

Brothers, let's be honest, we all know we can be crazy as a bedbug, short of three chromosomes. When we're not getting our way, that's when we do the most…

Smile or laugh… take a moment and process all of that. It was a lot, I know.

As you're going through your process and you've accepted there's no way around the courses you must pass through, your spirit is being strengthened, and so is your body.

You now see God is working on your behalf. Of course, the pain is still there. You, who's reading this, your pain hasn't subsided. You're trying to medicate the very thing you have no control over… your feelings.

As each day comes and goes, you're being met with something new. God told me, "This is a hard reset." I'll never forget those words. I remember calling my best bro and sharing with him what God said to me. I then heard, "Well, brother, you're gonna have to ride that out. You'll be fine" …

I called the covering friend and shared with her the same thing. She had the audacity to quickly say, "Kirby, I'm about to shower and head out. I'll call you back later tonight." She never did. She returned home at whatever time and went to bed. I reckon.

I'm thinking, what's happening!?

Best bro gave an answer. He was short, though…

My covering friend gave no answer…

I can't tell you what I uttered. Just know they were words fit for a Spades game!

Here are two power points I gathered. I'll share them with you. You're welcome!

Best bro trained me in spiritual calisthenics. I learned how to withstand. There was no need for him to continue to listen to unproductiveness. I knew exactly what to do!

My covering friend. She did her job and wouldn't interfere. It gave me everything I needed to continue to survive that season. Not only was I layered, but I was also concealed. I had to learn how to bud and blossom in a different type of environment.

The Juniper Tree is right where it's supposed to be. Your time will come, and you will know when to take refuge. I encourage you, brothers, don't overthink the process.

Don't avoid the journey. Every facet of the process and journey is only there to ensure you become who and what God has called you to be and to do.

Hebrews 12:12
Therefore, strengthen your feeble arms and weak knees.
Journaling Challenge.

On the blank pages, I challenge you to think about The Juniper Tree and all you read. Journal your thoughts. Later, you'll have something to read for self-encouragement or to share with someone else!

Let's finish 6 of those 12 characteristics of The Juniper Tree. Hopefully, the remaining ten will provoke your thoughts.

It's described as being full. This scripture comes to mind…

Psalm 16:11
Thou wilt shew me the path of life: in thy presence is fullness of joy; at thy right hand there are pleasures for evermore.

Your time spent underneath The Juniper Tree is a time for divine revelation.

While you're in your time of rest and recovery, it's vital to make sure your mind and spirit are settled. Ask God to show you exactly what you are to gain from being under The Juniper Tree.

While you're waiting for him to reveal, open your heart, your spirit, and your mind. Allow him to minister to those areas of brokenness.

He will replace your sadness with his joy. For every unwilling sacrifice you've made, he will give unto you treasures evermore.

Please understand this. When God speaks of treasures evermore, he's telling you what he's bringing into your life will last forever. This is an endless supply of abundance.

Writing each characteristic, I can't help but be triggered. In a great way that is.

Longevity is a major part of The Juniper Tree. God created it to live through seasons. Even the season that bears no fruit. No fruit doesn't speak to the health of the tree. It's still very active, and it gives everything it's responsible for.

This definitely describes my leader. Apostle Marlon Hester Sr. is such an outstanding man. His leadership qualities are unmatched.

His presence and voice all of last year were extremely vital to my survival, my coming out of that dark space, and my introduction to my next.

For the life of me, I couldn't see past my trauma. He had vision. And made it easy for me to be guided by his insight. He also gave language to every moment I faced.

Longevity speaks to assurance. I couldn't help but take a look at his life. All of what he had experienced and lived through became fuel in my mental engine.

I was assured daily. We literally talked every night during that season. I needed his voice. His prayers were refreshing. The prophetic declarations spoken over my life were on time.

He showed me beyond words that he wouldn't walk away or go by whatever he was told. His words were, "Son, can't nobody tell me anything that will make me turn my back on you. I stand with you."

AFFIRMATIONS ARE NECESSARY!

Perhaps you're in a space now and needing affirmation. Let me say this: there's absolutely nothing wrong with being affirmed. That's in fact a love language.

If you're not accustomed to being affirmed, adjust your mind, your way of thinking, and create space for someone to be that affirming voice you need.

Genuine Affirming Words is the glue that binds positive mental health in those areas where it's needed.

Romans 10:17
So, then faith cometh by hearing, and hearing by the word of God.

There are some brothers who have those feelings of inadequacy, due to the true fact that they were not affirmed by their fathers!

As we know, identity comes from the Father. A part of a man's identity is the way he's talked to and loved by his father.

My leader isn't just a spiritual leader. He's likened unto my Father. I call him "Pops." The stability, humility, and love for his wife and children are all enough for any man to model after.

"THE LIGHT BULB & SWITCH."

In January of 2016, I met this amazing couple from Tampa, Florida. At the time, I was living in North Carolina.

We were already connected via Social Media. But our official meeting was due to a post that I addressed on Facebook. I had no idea my commentary on a flyer would gain that much attention.

This couple reached out to me, and from there, a connection was made. We were ignorant of what the future held. It was promising, purposeful, and lifelong.

In January of that same year, they invited me to minister at their church. What an amazingly powerful 3-day event.

God showed himself in such a miraculous way. Even the youth and younger children were full participants in that awesome outpour.

One year later, it was established that I serve as their Apostolic Leader and Spiritual Father. Here we are, 10 years connected, and it's been an outstanding journey.

In December 2024, we didn't know the tables were turning against me. I found myself facing a harsh reality. I won't get into it here.

I'm writing a separate book from that. But I can share how it all interconnects with the totality of all that transpired.

The ending of 2024 and all of 2025, they were present, walking their leader through one of the most difficult seasons ever.

I'm being hit with lies. They were viciously horrible. To the point I wanted to come out of character. The narratives were countless.

Some of it now, I sit back and smile, and may even laugh a little. I walked out of 2025 with my whole mind. I had two amazing people, my son and daughter, who were there to make sure I remained focused!

As I've sat over the course of trying to decide how this book should be written, my mind often wandered about how to include them. As each chapter was written, it began to unfold.

The Juniper Tree. The 6 characteristics. And now that I'm here reading through the definitions of each word, for prophetic clarity, the picture is now clear.

Structure
Healing
Recovery

These 3 words are exactly what they ushered into my life. My son is a straightforward type of man. Particularly, he doesn't spend too much time in the explanation area. He gives direct insight and instructions.

My daughter is the one who spends the extra time. She laid down with me in the trenches. She didn't mind me throwing my dirt on her. I was spewing mental vomit on her. She didn't mind that either.

I was wearing her thin. She mentioned 3 times over the course of one year, "Apostle, I'm tired. But I'm not, I'm not gonna walk away. However, I have the answers you need. Stop fighting me. I'm not against you. Please know, I am for you."

What I love about their union is their sync. They understand each other's gifts and callings, aside from what they're called to do together as pastors.

As the journey of deconstruction began, my daughter signed up first. It wasn't planned. It was by conversation and because of a certain matter that had already taken place.

As she began to declutter my mind by speaking hard truths, I became like a toddler. Tantrum after tantrum. All of what she said during that time was the truth. Raw and uncut.

Some nights we'd talk 4-5 hours. I was missing important factors because I was too busy trying to prove my right and the other person's wrong.

Truth is, I was wrong. I was wrong because of who I was as a godly man. I didn't want to take accountability. I solely stood on facts and experience. I was dead in offense. I couldn't hear the truth. Neither could I see just how wrong I was.

One night on the phone with my daughter, the conversation lasted for hours. By the time the call ended, I hung up with a chip on my shoulder.

"Arrogance Will Cost You Little, To Lose What's Expensive And Irreplaceable."

Our next call was different. My son answered the call. He said to me...

"Apostle, I have a challenge. Go read and study Ephesians 5. Come back and let me know what God gave you."

I accepted the challenge with pride. Little did I know, he was setting me up for the kill. Ephesians 5 busted me down at least 7 notches.

Brothers, I want you to know that God never allows us to go through testing with a teacher who talks and gives out answers.

My son was that teacher. He avoided my combativeness on every angle. He simply gave the lesson and test.

When I released my pride, I was able to then strive with precision. The lesson was indeed thorough, but I passed that test. The revelation God gave me has had me in a chokehold since then.

As they walked with me, as they carried me through the year, their divine purpose in my life during that season was discovered.

It was no longer about me being their leader— but rather they being what I needed. I made space for them. I got out of the driver's seat. I took a backseat and let them take turns driving me through my journey.

Their role in my life during that appointed time and season had a triple effect.

- **Structure**. My son was the modeling example of structure. He had the language and lifestyle of structure. It was undeniable.

- **Recovery**. Together, both of them committed to ensuring that my recovery time would be healthy and that there wouldn't be any interruptions during the recovery process.

- **Healing**. The time frame of healing was according to my full participation. I had to condition my mind and accept what I couldn't change.

I want to elaborate on healing. My son and daughter refused to be on the side of my emotions, which were detrimental to my healing. They held me accountable.

What I didn't need to hear, they didn't utter. It's so very easy to manipulate anyone willing to only listen to your pity but never offer you the truth you need to overcome.

The "M&M" factor is a real thing.

Motive and Manipulation. Those who love you are often your weakest support. It's because the situation that has devastated you has impacted them.

So, they become blind to the truth of your error. They fall for your narratives. And although you may be telling the truth, the truth is they have to become numb to your soul-ish cry.

Paying attention all while strategically ignoring. They have to look at and listen to the factors that aren't being spoken about. The key to that is listening to you, telling how it's everybody else's fault.

And if you've never taken time to share the truth about your bad behaviors, those non-integral ways, things you've done and said that are all a part of what you have going on, time has been wasted completely.

Brothers, we need voices who will indeed listen, but we need voices that will check us, ask us the ground-breaking question— "what did you do"?

The Groundbreaking Factor.

Preparing for growth, the ground has to be broken. Grass is supposed to be green, but what's beneath is the big question!

When your life becomes the ground that is frequently visited, at some point and time, damage is being done.

When there's a shortage of boundaries, there's no order for parking. Those who know you hurt you without knowing it. You don't even know you're hurt. It's because we all go by what we see. The outer layers.

But what lies beneath tells the story. The internal you is the operating you. It's how you live totally. If you never take the time to zone your life, it'll always be friendly traffic.

I pastored for almost 9 years. Straight through. Never had a vacation, a break, adequate rest, or quality time to decompress. The list goes on.

Now that I'm in a different season of life, I'm able to see every error I made.

Self-Neglect
Physical Health Deprivation
Mental Starvation
Vision Without Language
A Gift. No Compass

The above is the rooting system. What lies beneath will always give proof of what's above. It's more than numbers. Far beyond "good church," the ability to stir the masses.

I was unhealthy and had no idea. I didn't take the time out to ever tell my inner man. The soil of my soul was terrible. There was growth but no trimmings. I didn't deal with the "tear" that lived amongst wheat. I was leading and greatly feeding those I served.

What was being given to the church, I wasn't replenishing myself. Genuine truth, I didn't know. I thought I was doing everything right.

By the time I realized that Groundbreaking needed to take place, it was too late. It was over. Desolation had become a thing. A hard thing.

The Groundbreaking Factor had to take place. My life without anything or anyone. Being busted up, the disconnecting of old roots. The soil had dried up. The wheat died out, but the tears remained. Left with absolutely nothing.

Brother, you've reached a groundbreaking moment. Let me tell you now, it's okay. Groundbreaking doesn't speak to a final ending. It's not over.

The moment is telling you of your value. There's life left in you. The voices that are current to help you heal and shift your focus away from fears, they're preparing you to be on new ground.

All of the digging and gutting out is painful. But what shall come forth will be what you have not been. Ever. Don't fight those voices of accountability, truth, and healing. Your recovery is priceless. Who you should become and what you should do will shift the trajectory of your life and purpose.

The Ground Breakers. They are there to examine you. Although they see the green, they're not impressed. They are present with tools. I encourage you to do as I did, let them get to work!

I'll leave you with this Groundbreaking scripture.

[highlight]

Hosea 10:12
Sow to yourselves in righteousness, reap in mercy; break up your fallow ground: for it is time to seek the Lord, till he come and rain righteousness upon you.

CHAPTER 11

"INVESTED VICTIMS"

I was chosen by my spiritual mother to succeed her in ministry as the next pastor of the church she founded. 25 years she has pastored.

From my understanding, her decision had been determined 10 years prior; I wasn't around. I was living in North Carolina.

I had zero intentions to ever return to live or pastor in my hometown. Not because it was bad, I just loved living away. I was busy traveling full-time as an itinerant preacher. I was away from the familiar!

November 13, 2016, on a Sunday morning, I had the honor to minister for my spiritual mother. The service was powerful. After the service, she pulled me into her office.

She asked me a question. "What would be the very first thing you would do as the next pastor of Restoration & Deliverance"?

I was confused because I was thinking to myself, " Why are you asking me this?" So, I said, "Huh." I thought about it, and my response was, "I'll fire everyone you currently have in place as leaders."

She asked me why. I answered that also. There were other things mentioned or talked about. Shortly afterwards, I left.

I want to bring you to my point without diving deep into the transition. One of the things she shared with me, as she relinquished her duties unto me...

"Son, I must tell you now. Don't let the sweet words of people get in your head or your heart. They will be the same people who will tear you down in the end. Remember, I told you first."

Those words never left me. I have to admit I absolutely loved those that I had the opportunity to lead. We experienced transformation, growth, and undeniable supernatural manifestations.

Great and soulful narratives are spoken by those who make up the congregation. Especially during certain moments, that's centered around the pastor.

Special occasions such as anniversaries, birthdays, and appreciations are the times the members have their opportunity to share their heartfelt expressions.

- **We have the best Pastor.**
- **Your leadership is worth following.**
- **The best/my favorite preacher**
- **Social media shoutouts**
- **I'm not leaving my church**

This list goes on. I heard it all over the course of 8 1/2 years. Some of it blessed me deeply. I found myself holding back tears. Transparent moment for a second; sometimes I would sit back and cringe on the inside, because I could see straight through a few of them. Depending upon my frame of mind at the time.

When the enemy crept in, he was able to gain control of our greatest defense in the spirit, our team of intercessors. That devil ran through those strong praying vessels.

In December of 2024, the prayer team had fallen apart. From there, we begin to experience hit after hit. I knew exactly what was happening. Because of my exhaustion, both physically and spiritually, I honestly didn't care.

It takes a while for me to develop the "I don't care" attitude, because I've done all I can. When enough is enough, then there's nothing more that can be said!

We all can reach this place of no return. And should we choose to not deal with any of it, it's pretty much a wrap. I reached that very place.

From there, the ministry went on a downward spiral. Each month, there were issues. All the way til the closing of the doors.

The next BIG THING to hit me was when I began seeing the disrespect via social media. The shade was above my pay grade.

Instead of tagging names with my responses, I took notes. I filtered through all of what was being said and shared.

It wasn't until I gained revelation. Something profound was spoken to me, and my perspective changed. A bright light shone within the core of my soul.

I changed my frown into a smile. On purpose. I could have responded via social media. I could have confronted them directly. But for what?

There was absolutely nothing there to gain from any of it. I sorted through the trash, but nothing was worth taking or keeping.

Here's what I gathered. It sounded like a bell sitting in the church tower…

"Every losing investor makes noise."

During my time of journaling, I wrote my thoughts, I shared my feelings, I wrote a song, and I penned a poem. I reminded myself of the importance of my silence during that season.

I stayed committed to the cause of my journey. I was in a "one-man marathon." The sideline audience was people who knew Kirby. The dude that wasn't afraid of anything, that didn't back down or walk away from adversity.

Brothers, this is the grit you must have. Doing the total opposite of what you're accustomed to and being who you haven't been— the one they don't know.

There's a greater you, and you're being reborn and shaped into who and what God has ultimately called for.

INVESTED VICTIMS

They are the very people who once said all the great things about you. They loved you, stood with you, supported you, said they would ride for you, gifted you, and made it known to the world. But now that you've hit ROCKBOTTOM, you're now nothing. You're the complete opposite of what they once said and did.

I guess they all forgot!?

In the world of social media, one of the strongest parts is RECEIPTS!
Those memories surface to serve as a reminder of not only what was said, but also to remind you of who you are.

As I end this short chapter, I want you to know, it's not over for you. Some things have ended just to introduce you to a new beginning. Say hello to Fear. Let it be made known you're not hiding,

YOU'RE OUTSIDE. NOTHING CAN STOP YOU. YOU'RE ALL THE WAY UP!!!

Isaiah 40:10
So do not fear, for I am with you; do not be dismayed, for I am your God. I will strengthen you and help you; I will uphold you with my righteous right hand.

CHAPTER 12

ROCKBOTTOM HAS A BASEMENT

The Foundation of All Things New

Brothers, I want to first thank you for your mental endurance. You took the time to read this manifesto.

It's my prayer that you've gained something from it that you can take with you as you continue to journey through life.

I want to share that hitting ROCKBOTTOM wasn't an easy thing. Neither was it planned. I had no expectations for the events I had to face.

When I realized nothing was changing as I felt it should, I chose to buckle down and treat the journey as a rodeo rider.

I determined in my mind that I was gonna ride it out until the end. I refused to give up or die. I expressed how certain people were positioned strategically.

You may be in the slums of life. You're reading this because you're still breathing. That means your life isn't over. Yes, you've lost much. I will not minimize your truth. But I will say this: whatever you've lost, you can certainly recover.

The Foundation of All Things New.

Foundation - the solid base or groundwork supporting a structure.

Once you have removed the debris of what's left of your life, take a look at yourself. Let me tell you what you're looking at: YOU. You are your greatest foundation.

You now have the divine opportunity to rebuild your life as God intended and as you so desire.

The betrayal, the heartbreak, the lies, the terrible narratives, the scandal, the public tabloids, etc.

They must become building blocks. One of my hardest lessons was learning how to make the negative press work for my good.

The truth is, it was hard for me to see value in what was bad. It all had a foul purpose. To break me. I couldn't see past it.

The labyrinth of my mind made it extremely difficult to process. Unanswered question. Even now, I must be honest, I have questions that haven't received answers. Lots of them.

Am I to remain stuck? Hesitant about my next move? Hell no! I had to get up. It wasn't anyone's job to make me stand up and be the man I am.

You are your foundation. You're worthy of a new beginning. You definitely survived what has taken many out of here!

I challenge you to get it in. I want you to start and finish strong. I want to help you by sowing into your mental, language that serves as a compass for you.

Your Framework.

This is where you began to fortify the important factors about your life.

- **Skeletal System of your life. You began the mental wiring process.**

– Rules [external]
– Boundaries [internal]
– Structure
– Principles
– Ideas
– Permanent Self Guide [brain of your heart]

As you're rebuilding your life, I encourage you not to be in a hurry. Take your time and ensure you leave nothing out.

You do not want to repeat what you've conquered and outlived.

The Basement in real time is often used as a workspace. It's the place where projects are started and finished.

The Basement represents privacy. I learned this and made it work for me. Moving forward, I chose to make it work for me.

I'm a critical thinker. And, being that my life became a public spectacle, I decided to rob the public of my physical presence. I made my misery my fortress.

I taught myself to make Privacy work for me. I began working. I'm now focused and rebuilding my life.

There was once a time when I would think about a project but not start it.
I have a driven and untampered passion to do what I know to do. I have reasons not to. I have nothing hindering me. Nothing is a distraction.

You're able to read this book because I wrote in Privacy. In fact, two books have been written in private.

The Basement will work for you if you learn and come to know how to make it work for you. It may be dark there, but turn the light on. It may be too quiet. Turn on some music. A sound with meaningful words that will ease your mind and speak life to your heart and spirit.

Brick by Brick

After the completion of the skeletal system, use the best bricks to wall up your life. What are those bricks you may ask!?

- **Survival**
- **Lessons**
- **Application**
- **Determination**
- **Skills**
- **New-found abilities**
- **Knowledge**
- **Wisdom**
- **Faith**
- **God's Word**
- **Prayer**
- **Focus**

Brother, you're a Master Builder! As you carefully rebuild, there's a momentum resting upon you. Excitement is normal, and it's great, but don't let it slow you down. Stay in the grind. God has given you grit that's on steroids.

Most importantly, don't share until you're finished. Sometimes talking a little too much invites unnecessary attention and negativity that you didn't sign up for.

Nehemiah 6:3
But I realized they were plotting to harm me, so I replied by sending this message to them: "I am engaged in a great work, so I can't come. Why should I stop working to come and meet with you?"

Locked In.

Now that you're locked in, begin to decompress from your labor. Much labor was put forth. I want you to know, brother, I am proud of you.

Allow me to point out your labor. You'll have solid proof of your tenacity and the quality of a man you are!

- **labor of survival**
- **labor of recovery**
- **labor of healing**
- **labor of restoration**
- **labor of new beginnings**

Brother, I survived, you survived, and we're both here to share our moment with those who deserve our time. Here's my final thing I have to share with all of you…

Remember this. As you move forward to LIVE AGAIN, please do so with intentional happiness. But also, do so with the greatest part of you. Those that call you dad, uncle, cousin, coach, mentor, Mr., and friend....

Leave behind your LEGACY. Some generations will benefit from what you've worked so hard to accomplish and establish.

Proverbs 13:22
A good man leaves an inheritance to his children's children, but the sinner's wealth is laid up for the righteous.

Your role as a Father may extend outside of your natural biology, and it's okay. You may be the father figure to many. That's great too. In all you do, be sure to make an impact that will last, even after you have expired!

The end.

THE BASEMENT

A 10-Day Devotional

Day 1: Foundation Matters

Scripture: ***Matthew* 7:24**

A strong life is never built overnight. It is formed through consistent decisions, daily discipline, and a commitment to truth. Many men chase success, money, or recognition, believing those things will secure their future.

But when pressure comes, those things alone cannot hold you up.

Jesus compares life to building a house. The difference between stability and collapse is not the storm, it is the foundation. Storms come to everyone. The question is whether your life is rooted in something unshakable.

A solid foundation is built through obedience, not just knowledge. Hearing the truth is not enough. Applying it daily is what creates strength. Small, consistent actions over time produce a life that can withstand anything.

As a man, you are building something every day: your character, your habits, your legacy. The foundation you choose today determines the outcome tomorrow.

Take time to evaluate what your life is truly built on. Remove anything unstable and replace it with principles that endure.

Day 2: Discipline Over Feelings

Scripture: ***1 Corinthians 9:27***

Discipline is one of the defining traits of a strong man. Feelings come and go, but discipline remains steady. If you rely on motivation, you will often fall short. But if you build discipline, you create consistency.

An athlete trains regardless of how they feel. They understand that growth comes from repetition, effort, and pushing beyond comfort. The same applies to life. Growth requires doing what is necessary, even when it is difficult.

Discipline impacts every area: your health, your mindset, your relationships, and your purpose. Without it, potential is wasted. With it, ordinary effort becomes extraordinary results.

Every time you choose discipline over comfort, you strengthen your character. Over time, these choices define who you become.

Start small. Build daily habits that align with the man you want to be.

____

____

Day 3: Lead Yourself First

Scripture: ***Proverbs 16:32***

Leadership begins within. Before you can guide others, you must first master yourself. Many men desire influence but lack self-control. True leadership is not about power; it is about responsibility.

Your emotions, thoughts, and actions must be aligned. If you cannot control your temper, your impulses, or your decisions, you will struggle to lead effectively.

Self-leadership requires awareness. You must recognize your weaknesses and actively work to improve them. This takes humility and commitment.

When you lead yourself well, others will naturally trust and follow you. Your example becomes your influence.

Focus on becoming the kind of man who leads by example, not just words.

____

____

____

____

____

Day 4: Integrity When No One Is Watching

Scripture: ***Proverbs 10:9***

Integrity is the foundation of trust. It is not built in public but in private moments when no one else sees your choices. A man of integrity does what is right, regardless of the cost. He does not compromise his values for convenience or approval.

Your character is revealed in the small decisions you make daily. Over time, those decisions shape your reputation and your legacy.

Living with integrity brings peace. You do not have to hide, pretend, or fear being exposed. Commit to honesty in all areas of your life, even when it is difficult.

____

____

____

____

____

____

____

____

Day 5: Strength Through Humility

Scripture: ***James 4:10***

Humility is often misunderstood as weakness, but it is actually a form of strength. It takes confidence to admit when you are wrong and courage to seek growth.

Pride prevents progress. It convinces you that you already know enough or that you do not need help. Humility opens the door to learning and improvement.

Strong men are teachable. They listen, learn, and grow from others.

When you humble yourself, you position yourself for elevation. Growth follows humility. Practice humility by staying open to correction and committed to growth.

____

____

____

____

____

____

____

____

Day 6: Guard Your Mind

Scripture: ***Romans 12:2***

Your mind is one of your greatest assets. What you allow into it will shape your thoughts, decisions, and actions. Negative influences, distractions, and unhealthy patterns can slowly weaken your mindset. Guarding your mind requires intentional choices.

Replace harmful input with things that build you, truth, wisdom, and positive influence.

A renewed mind leads to a transformed life. Change begins internally before it shows externally. Be intentional about what you consume daily.

____

____

____

____

____

____

____

____

____

Day 7: Responsibility Is Power

Scripture: ***Luke 16:10***

Responsibility is not a burden; it is an opportunity. How you handle what is in front of you determines what comes next. Many men want more but are not managing what they already have. Growth requires stewardship. When you take full ownership of your life, you step into power. Excuses fade, and progress begins. Small responsibilities prepare you for larger ones. Handle them well.

Choose ownership in every area of your life.

____

____

____

____

____

____

____

____

____

____

____

Day 8: Control Your Words

Scripture: ***Proverbs 18:21***

Words carry weight. They can build confidence or destroy it. As a man, what you say matters deeply. Speaking with intention requires awareness and discipline. Not every thought needs to be spoken.

Use your words to encourage, guide, and uplift others. Your voice should bring clarity, not confusion; strength, not fear. Be mindful of your speech and its impact.

Day 9: Perseverance Builds Character

Scripture: ***James 1:12***

Life will test you. Challenges are not optional; they are part of growth.

Perseverance is what separates those who succeed from those who quit. It builds resilience and strength.

Every obstacle is an opportunity to grow stronger.

Do not give up when things get hard. That is often where growth is happening.

Stay committed, even in difficult seasons.

Day 10: Leave a Legacy

Scripture: ***Proverbs 13:22***

Your life has a lasting impact. The choices you make today shape the future for others. Legacy is not just about wealth; it is about values, character, and influence.

What you model will be remembered. Live intentionally. Think beyond today. Build something that lasts beyond your lifetime. Commit to becoming a man whose life leaves a positive mark.

CONTACT THE AUTHOR

To contact the author for book speaking engagements, bulk purchases, or comments, please reach out to:

(Dr. Kirby Gant)

Email **(prophetkgant@yahoo.com)**

Social Media Facebook @ KirbyGant
X: @ K_DrGant
Instagram: @KirbyGant

www.ingramcontent.com/pod-product-compliance
Lightning Source LLC
LaVergne TN
LVHW010835120826
845149LV00016B/2466
* 9 7 9 8 9 8 9 4 2 9 5 5 4 *